Rough Ascension

and Other Poems of Science

Rough Ascension

and Other Poems of Science

Arthur J. Stewart

Celtic Cat Publishing

KNOXVILLE, TENNESSEE

Published by Celtic Cat Publishing
Knoxille, Tennessee
www.celticcatpublishing.com

Acknowledgments

Special thanks to Jim Johnston and Marilyn Kallet for graciously providing the guidance, critical eye, and deft touch. The author also thanks the editors of the following magazines, journals and anthologies, where some of the poems and essays in this collection have appeared:

Bulletin of the Ecological Society of America; Lullwater Review; Eclectic Literary Forum; All Around Us: Poems from the Valley; Songs from Unsung Worlds: Science 85; and *Quantum Tao.*

Manufactured in the United States of America
Design by Dariel Mayer
Cover art by Justin A. Dickerman-Stewart
Back cover photograph by Aaron J. Stewart

ISBN 0–9658950–5-X
Library of Congress Control Number: 2003106579

Technological Progress

Digging Out

Rough Ascension

Dissecting Time

For Gus—
and those who love science

On the Need for Poetry by Scientists

Two contributions to *Science* magazine—a news report by Glanz (1997), titled "Cut the Communications Fog, Say Physicists and Editors," and a letter to the editor by Emmert (1997), titled "Poets, Painters, and the Future of Science," provide fodder for the idea that simple communication problems are significant obstacles to science. These contributions also support the idea that scientists may benefit directly and indirectly by stronger efforts to protect and encourage creativity in its multiple forms, and that the public, in turn, might benefit by helping scientists better understand the value of creativity, a force that underpins both the arts and the sciences. In short, points raised in the articles mentioned above lead me to believe that a strong argument can be made for the need to help close the divide between art and science, on practical grounds. But I do not try to make this argument here, because arguments inherently tend to be polarizing and divisive. Rather, my objective is that of trying to nudge art and science a little closer by offering something tangible, something closer to the heart.

Recent personal experience suggests that voids in communication between the two ends of the creative spectrum are greater than most scientists might imagine—but perhaps not so great as most poets seem to suspect. Professionally, I function as an environmental scientist, with expertise in aquatic ecology and ecotoxicology. However, I also write and publish poetry in literary magazines. Such odd and interesting bedfellows, these two things! At a meeting several years ago, I was bold enough to tell an audience of scientists that an award that I had recently earned for one poem was ". . . logistically, about ten times more difficult to achieve than National Science Foundation funding . . ." The statement got a good laugh, but it remains true. And in the scientist-infested hallways of Oak Ridge National Laboratory, when I showed a coworker a serious poem I had written, the professional response was, "That's cute!". In this age of specialization and scientific rigor, perhaps we have come too far. Or perhaps, I suggest, not far enough, on issues relating aesthetics to science. But how are we to determine this, and what might we do about it?

Here, in my first formal attempt to bridge poetry and science from the science shore, I offer two poems addressing uncertainties that I have encountered while contemplating the need for bridge-building, and give a brief personal commentary on each.

What They Found

They found
telomerase in a cell
adding bits
of DNA to the ends

of chromosomes,
thus compensating
for losses that occur
with routine cell division

which means

could we live forever ageless?

Learning

My nine and duckling students dear—
I cannot teach you how iron-weed
by slamming purple softens
the wild hills in autumn.

So on this bold day I say just
iron-weed blooms, and dig in
stitching raw pieces of data with statistics,
explaining the need to round to whole
near numbers, values that have clear meaning.

But when I look up at last
I must stop and lean forward, learning
in your young eyes
how beautifully these tumbling
fragments of knowledge adorn you.

One should understand that although I am a practicing scientist, I know almost nothing about telomerase, other than what I have read in *Science* magazine or heard on National Public Radio. And sadly, my knowledge of simple cell division now is scarcely deeper than the veneer I acquired as an undergraduate student, years ago. But the poem "What They Found" is not really about telomerase at all, so this technical deficit doesn't matter much. Telomerase, in this case, is merely a convenient metaphor for a deeper issue of science itself. What one finds, in asking any good scientific question, inevitably is a path leading to another question only. And *that's* what the "they" in the poem really found: a new question, imbued with its own plethora of ethical and moral issues—a question about the possibility of learning to significantly extend the length of human life. To foster a sense of quick and breathless discovery (which is, I'm sorry to report, too rarely achieved!), line length in the poem is kept short and the entire poem is but a single sentence. An element of surprise is established by spatially isolating the last line of the poem from the preceding stanza.

In "Learning," a twist in perspective is used to highlight the development of personal understanding acquired about teaching and science, while teaching a class in biology. The truth is, there is much we don't know scientifically about how iron-weed ". . . by slamming purple softens / the wild hills in autumn. . . ," because the aesthetics of nature extend almost infinitely beyond our primitive ability to write equations, and human perception is deeper than any tools that science offers. Anyone who has taught some aspect of science knows the sense of frustration that comes from trying to teach, using only the tools of science. One must teach the tools of science, I think, and help students *see* the science to which these tools can be applied. And when ". . . I look up at last / I must stop and lean forward, learning . . . ," the message is complete, encapsulated and installed: I realize, in that jumbled precious instant, that at least one of the students also realizes that the facts are only tools. By this, the bond is created. I see then, in that instant, that *I* have learned, from the very students that I am trying to teach. In that instant, I sincerely appreciate ". . . how beautifully these tumbling / fragments of knowledge adorn you."

I review many technical manuscripts per year, on topics ranging from soil chemistry to the ecological monitoring of mosses in streams. The opportunity to inspect these products of science is enlightening. In an autopsy, the science-beast's soft underbelly, once slit open, is expected to reveal to the reader a defined set of interactive organs, positioned in a particular way: introduction, materials and methods, results, discussion, references, tables and figures. These organs are expected to be clear, separate, and concise, yet function together. They should be rationally linked, organically dynamic, and bend to the needs established and driven specifically by the research question. Unfortunately, in a large majority of cases,

> These manuscripts
> waft in, gasping and under the knife
> I find them
> wet creatures with three eyes,
>
> unable to see, data-infested
> spleens wrapping livers, intestines
> connected to the lungs,
> dysfunctional, going nowhere
>
> and the heart
> motionless.

In my experience, scientists account for the greatest portion of the gulf between science and the arts, and it is scientists that may have the most to gain if this situation can be remedied. Ultimately, a truth can be expressed by simple speaking, raised exactingly from the heart. But due to human perceptual and language limitations, many truths can be expressed and assimilated as metaphors, similes, and analogies more easily than they can be expressed in unvarnished technical form. Furthermore, the structure of science depends on the identification and exploration of cause and effect, yet bits of scientific truth that we uncover are rarely complete enough to raise from the heart in intact form. Instead, they are more often mined as fragments or discovered as shards, and must be organized and positioned later if they are to contribute meaningfully to the body of science.

The ideas above lead me to suggest that it may be particularly important for scientists to become more comfortable and accepting of the use of metaphors, analogies, and similes in their work, and to be willing to incorporate these, as appropriate, into the way they think. Clear organization, a compelling logic-path for the presentation of ideas, the effective supporting of those ideas by data, and austerity and precision in use of language emerge more easily once a compelling metaphor has been defined.

I have seen reference before to classes taught by scientists, under the title "Science for Poets." In such classes, non-science majors are provided the rudiments of science. What may benefit us more, though, is a mandatory course on Poetry for Scientists, taught by poets—and an appreciation, by scientists, that poets have something more to offer than words alone, a deeper thing.

———

Glanz, J. 1997. Cut the communications fog, say physicists and editors. *Science* 277: 895–96.

Emmert, M. A. 1997. Poets, painters, and the future of science. *Science* 278: 1381.

Technological Progress

Technological Progress

I tell my sons, you must learn
to insinuate yourself into the world:
you must learn to work
in, amongst and through

the molecularity of being; you must learn
how to push the delicate
threads of the self into pixels,
energy fields, Gaussian curves, the step-

functions of life; you must
come to understand uncertainty,
the silly prancing dance of neutrons,
electrons, and learn how to surf

advances in new materials: blue lasers,
solid-state biphasic epsilonic wavelets,
quantum computing, nano-scale fabrication:
a propensity of density,

oh yes, wonderful things
beyond my comprehension. It's time
I say for your dad to fall
behind the curve. And don't forget

I say to love.

Weaver's Needle

Do not dangle your participles or split infinitives,
my wild-haired high-school English teacher said.
She could build sentences from the cool dry breeze
that worked the walls of the ragged canyons

deep in the Superstition Mountains, where even now
the red sun dips behind the Weaver's Needle.
Do not, she said,
use words you do not know.

Never circle a clean center with fuzz.
Her voice, we said,
quivered like the call of a thin coyote,
adding nearly nothing to the morning air.

Now my skin tingles, my ear strains
for the last trembling note of her. She leans
forward in my memory: her gold wire-rim glasses rest
precariously upon the narrow bridge of her thin nose.

She's serious; she puts her stare
hard to each of us trying to teach us
something fundamental.
We sit, dolts, hopeless even by our own accounting.

One of us might become something useful—
somehow, someday, by accident, or luck
or divine intervention. She hesitates,
building a web of love in her mind as we sit,

our thoughtless little heads bowed
in acquiescence, incapable of learning
but appreciative of her attempt to teach us
things she thought had value.

After class that day we filed out
silent, one after another, ragamuffin whipped.
But in the school's locker-lined hall
we soon gathered the strength of youth again:

safe in that brick canyon
with familiar metal echoes,
we lined up three deep and howled
like coyotes.

Juncos in Disequilibrium

November settles down at last
snapping cold wet
leaves off trees. Blackbirds
flew south last week; a few juncos

just in from the north
ahead of the storm
bounce among bushes. Each flashes
a pair of white-edged feathers

on a slender tail.
Watching them now I think back
to this morning—tail-feather memory
about a dog, or a wily creature like a dog,

quicker, leaner, more dangerous,
slinking the edge of the woods.
With this thought I find myself
lost, looking for specifics

among generalizations.
I search for a way to move forward
smoothly, steering among
fragments of silence.

I dig down to molecules,
each of which knows nothing
more than its own existence;
imagine I see them

looking at each other
over hypothetical shoulders,
Heisenbergian, busy gnashing
tiny teeth; finally they shimmer

to reluctant agreement—
enough, at least, to line up and hold hands
electrostatically speaking:
long enough, anyway,

to make keratin, shafts, hooks, barbels,
feather-pieces, colors, bits of bone, a tendon,
a drop of warm blood here,
a beak there, a bright eye,

yes, bringing, oh,
such temporary closure to juncos—
each different;
each in disequilibrium;

each proud of that pair of white-edged
feathers in the perky little tail.

Writing Plan for September

This, I say, making a mark,
will be my scrap-pile of work for the week.
I shall step it off daily
like estimates of hose-length

paced off in the yard;
I shall make progress each day,
sometimes as knots,
perhaps as smooth lines

moving like waves under steady wind,
systematic, tenacious
life digging itself out of the mold,
dirt clinging to the roots of trees.

Molecular Knowing

In *Science* magazine today
investigators busy themselves

unraveling the functions of genes.
They're looking for one that turns on

Sonic Hedgehog and others
with acronymic names

regulating molecular clocks
and transcriptional cascades.

"Signal transduction" is hot;
they close in on understanding

the cause of a cancer.
Knowing is upon us.

Superstring Theory

Rests on convoluted
ten-dimensional arguments with three
exposed, and the remaining
seven folded up in themselves

to a size no bigger than ten to the minus
33 centimeters, requiring 20 million times
more energy than that which can be produced
in the highest-energy particle colliders available,

just to see if

forces are tied at the core or can unite.
Relax the assumptions a bit,
suddenly everything makes sense:

the weak force
unites with gravity,
flowers bloom,
professors dance.

My Heart Aches

Yesterday, understanding emerged
from an experiment like a white lily opening,
slow, sweet and elegant. All day, euphoric,
I thrummed drunk with purity.

Now my head throbs with another chore.
I sit at my desk reviewing a report.
Malodorous road-kill distasteful
even to flies; prepared
by some BS consultant,
butcher of fact, unable to dot
his eyes or cross his knees.

It is stuffed
with cheap reason, built
from flawed thoughts—a slap-dash effort
tied hastily to a few weak references.

My pen bleeds, my heart aches
for the lily.

Relax, I say, relax.

I shake myself awake and pour
a cup of coffee; I clear the desk and take on
chapter two.

I create a clean hypothesis.
We grow, I say, scientifically
like an oyster grows its shell:

one thin layer at a time;
by adding small details;
by close attention;
by careful avoidance of platitudes.

Sublimation

The direct
conversion of ice
to vapor, bypassing
the molecular joy of water.

Small Things

In *Science* magazine today I learn about
microtubule-based actuators—devices in which
tiny applications of electrical current cause ions
put into a nannotube to jump

to the inside walls and bind there,
temporarily creating a double
electrostatic shell, which causes
structural deformation of the tube,

making it contract. Behaving, in short,
like a tiny artificial muscle.
These are very small things indeed
and may allow fabrication of micro-devices

capable of moving, or of containing
smaller parts that move and which require
almost no power. Now what
I wonder will they think of next?

Find the Core and Test the Wall for Strength

1.

At Chernobyl, reactor room 305 is filled
with fiercely radioactive slag
plus 190 tons of corium,
a mix of metal, concrete and graphite rods

melted to a man-made mess of a mass
giving off
more than thirty-five hundred rads per hour,
a blazing storm of radiation

capable of frying
electronic chips in seconds.
Even hardy robots fail a bleak, simple mission:
find the core and test the wall for strength.

2.

In *Science* magazine I learn that now they think
neutrinos may have a little mass, too:

perhaps a billionth as much as an electron,
or perhaps a little less,

it is hard to say for sure: they weigh
so little the mass must be inferred

indirectly, a sideways look at a tiny
bump on a chart.

3.

Ghostly things small as neutrinos
fly through me in the night.
I feel them
slipping through my core.

I lie awake in the dark
looking up at blackness only,
sensing a tiny pulse of life,
scarcely breathing.

Into this nightmare,
blind as a robot
sent to test the wall for strength,
I fall, failing.

Looking for Links

1.

Sometimes it takes a long time
turning stones, listening
for the quiet buzz or hum
of what to write.

On a bad day I can work for hours
yet not find one
sweet Mariam.

The cranky cat keeps walking
around the pond casually
eyeing the bug-eyed fish. The useless dog

sleeps on her special place,
crushing grass in the yard.

And I flip from book to book
looking for the exact flavor
I crave to no avail.

2.

I can't tell you
how an idea comes in finally
through the fingers, trickling down
or through the belly, working up.

When it does
I can get busy
ripping out commas and moving walls
though I must get up and walk around

often. I must keep looking, you know,
for links.

3.

Outside, a drought, so I water the trees.
That's the best way I know to cause it to rain.

Small oceans of dry leaves
and the ground under the dead leaves

cracks so little mouths drink.
I think about the volcano Parícutin

coming up in a corn field in Mexico, starting off
a small crack in the ground, like this, letting out

a trickle of smoke. There, at least,
finally it rumbled.

4.

When the rain comes at last
it drives. The grasses bend
to the will of water and the ground's many mouths
drink to thirst satisfied.

Inside Out

I could turn myself
inside out today—how curious! I've no clue
where this thought came from or why
it popped suddenly into my head.

Perhaps it has something to do
with microbial batteries, an idea
explained backwards to me yesterday
by a comrade in molecular detail,

pointing his stubby finger
to Kreb's-cycle products on the board.
What if, he said, we put the gene
for rhodopsin, a bacterial solar-driven proton pump,

into an anaerobic bacterium, say
Closeridium, then feed it
hydrogen and electrons:
would it make more butanol? He counted

electron equivalents, scratched
his head, put numbers to paper, thought
out loud, well, yes, it might be so.

2.

Massive reorganization
on the lab's horizon: the plan is,
we should turn ourselves
inside out. Use dollars

to power this pump—extrude managers,
re-write procedures, establish
new rules for business,
clarify objectives.

God help us
define the lab's mission
subject to Department of Energy approval,
of course. Some things don't change.

3.

Still, it devolves to a question,
how to get from here to there—
protons move under pressure
through semi-permeable membranes
by way of membrane-bound proteins;
managers move under peculiar pressures
of finance and administration,
what's the difference? We know

not much about each. I note if you tilt
the head back several degrees and roll
the eyes up to look at a cloud on high
it generates

a peculiar sense of motion in the head.

Long Haul

It is autumn: first yellow leaves
rest on short grass
under trees in the yard. Last night
they fell perfectly around the tulip poplar's

zone of vegetative influence, not yet
scattering far: leptokurtic—
that's the word for it: meaning,
more or less,

more closer to the source, and less
farther away. An outcome described
by a double power function
I don't pretend to understand: it works,

that's the important thing. It works
in the sense that with the right equation
one can predict
generally where the leaves will fall. Except

the damned wind: when it comes
it makes everything a mess and then
biologists and engineers run
in circles and it becomes clear

you can throw the equation
right out the window
for all the specific good it can do.
Truth is, in the short run,

the leaves will go
where the wind chooses;
like us, they go into the earth
over the long haul.

Why It Is So Difficult
for a Biologist to Write Poetry

1.

He might begin with the purple-blue
of an iris in spring, the color
that can't hold back—it wants
so much to lunge out of the wet earth from tubers
the first few days the air is warm.

He might begin with gray,
color of the alert mother-dove
absolutely motionless
on her two precious eggs, these being
held delicately in a nest
built hastily of twigs on a dogwood
branch not too high—an advantageous site
overlooking the yard, the tree
and the iris, of course,
shooting from the stony bed.

2.

But then he starts to wonder,
where's the truth? If it is early enough for iris
is it too early for a dove to nest and oh by the way
what's the condition of the tree—has it
put out its leaves, and if so
are they small as mouse-ears
or full-blown? And thus in an instant
the whole damned thing comes down, ruined.

No smoke or rubble,
but ruined completely nonetheless
although it is possible
two perfect little eggs did not get broken.

Production

In a smoky foundry lean men stoke fires,
sweating orange sparks gush
from grinding wheels, hard sounds
cut to the bone and sharp metal things

get made, polished, inspected, boxed, labeled,
shipped—they fly out over the land
to a thousand stores. They hold
warm places on shelves

while I work to put a flurry of words
out to die like birds on snow,
clinging briefly to high weeds
bending under a chill wind.

Digging Out

Katydids at Night

The world conceived in gray and green
comes out of the forest at dusk
getting darker, dragging cool air
and the rasping calls of katydids, each one
invisible but loud.
Their noisy stridulation is not a simple
shaping of the night the way lilacs
soften the edges of everything we hear;
it is not a simple punctuation,
like the careful chirps of crickets
from the deep grass: no, the katydids
chafe out their fears,
their long antennae slender
and thrown back over their folded-leaf
soft green bodies as they cling
to the need for love.

Ditching

"Put the deep trench where it wants to go",
Roy would say with his voice
coming from the place we couldn't see
under the beard. His upper face smoothed

thirty years by rain. He wasn't one for much
talking when the Ditch-Witch wanted to work.
He called her Sal and guided her
according to the way the dirt spoke. For hours

watching the endless stream of metal jaws
go forward, plunging themselves
into the loam and coming out
sparkling in sun, putting sweet dirt

safe to the side, sometimes the engine coughing
a little dark smoke when the blades
broke a root or caught a rock.
Ed and I would come in behind

laying schedule-forty PVC pipe,
kicking knots of grass to the side,
stepping sometimes on white grubs.
By noon with the sweat soaking our shirts

we were ready to take a break,
eat cheese and apples and drink Coke.
Roy's secret mouth worked
then like a mouse under hair, sometimes

giving a glimpse of teeth. Beside me
a grub—white body curled fat and glistening,
almost translucent, smooth brown head
bent as though in prayer. Could it see

through dirt or smell or feel the sun?
It scarcely moved in its dreams
even when I dribbled Coke on it,
brown liquid fizzing a moment

on the dirt as Roy sat working his jaws,
chewing, eyes closed, steady as a machine.

Beautiful Fish

After catching two small trout
casting with flies, the last of the sun
speckled them more and we walked
carrying them over stones as dusk slipped

among willows where the Delores River
slipped among stones. We cut
willow whips, stripped them and pushed
their pointed ends through the fish

mouth to tail and hung them
over a small fire roasting,
a few drips sputtering
now and then making sparks

jump in the smoke. We ate
those beautiful fish, peeling back
blackened skin
picking white flesh from delicate bones

between head and tail.
And they gave the river to us
completely that night, and the sky
peeled back too, giving stars.

Bison Zone

When we were done we left
Bartlesville, Oklahoma
driving seventy most of the way south
towards Tulsa in a cool white car
looking out at short oaks and the lowest hills
you can imagine. Day before
we had taken the time
to go north, turning left and right
into the tall-grass prairie, looking for bison.
We found them finally and stopped

there on the gravel road. Far off,
the loose herd, perhaps two hundred
with spring calves brown and the big guys
shaggy dark. They did not move much; they stirred
less than the wind rippled
the grasses. The quiet was deep enough to hold us,
and deep enough to make
a scissors-tail flycatcher sit motionless
on a high wire by the roadside.
The wind moved
shadows of high cumulus clouds
across low hills.

Seeing

The oaks have lost their hiding leaves
and through the clutter of bare trunks
and ragged limbs the occasional pond
nestles like a chilled wet thief in the hills.

In this season of seeing I hear
the mutter of wind through rough weeds
and rattle-leaves, and the voice of one
crying in this wilderness.

On this leather day with my camel-coat
flapping the wind and my bold red tie flying
in exuberance to my shoulder,
I along the paved road walk, wondering:

if I let my hair grow tangling
and cast off this coat and step
out of these shining shoes
could I become that wild

green man in autumn barefoot,
eating locusts, tasting the rich
lather of fermenting honey—
could I feel the hard storm coming and see

more clearly than I see now?

The Grand Canal

(Arizona; June, 1967)

I was seventeen and already wise
to the hazards of rum a little so we drove
at night a dozen miles bouncing only half-crocked
to the Grand Canal, near the base

of the Estrella Mountains rising
close enough to shut out
stars to the south
        and lord

in that solid blackness we made a small fire
there on the dirt road and sat and listened
to the water run and run
and to the burning wood

snapping. Occasionally
a rhinoceros beetle
half the size of a young girl's clenched fist
flew in roaring

like a bomber out of the darkness
attracted to the fire's light
making us dodge and curse in fear,
rum or no rum. Hours later:

fire's down to coals in the crisp air
and the eastern sky lightens to pink.
I'm on my back on the hard ground
snugged deep in a cheap sleeping bag

reeking of smoke, looking up
oblivious to the future, enjoying
now, the last stars.

Digging Out

All day the snow came down
a fury of flakes
covering the dead ground deep.

And the night
seemed same as the day
but dark.

And when I next woke
there was nothing to do
but dig out.

Knee-deep
each step was its own
special thing.

The truck was a mound
and only the tips of our little spruces
peeked above snow-line.

Each shovel-full of snow
cast up in the rhythm of digging out
made me arch, too,

labor of love under an intense
blue sky.

Great Blue Heron

On Sunday, this day
being Sunday, the heavy air
gloomy with cold as I drive
my truck with its inside air

warm and the radio low,
near the place where the road dips
past the school in a small hollow
someone dug out years ago, a place

grassed over so the trickle of stream
pools up, making a slick
silvery surface of water, reflecting
bare branches of a few dogwoods

and a large willow with half
its yellowing leaves gone;
suddenly I see there
at the shallow-water edge

where the willow's weak shadow
meets the bleak bank,
the lean gray body of a Great Blue Heron
motionless, waiting

for the glitter of a minnowy fish.

Tornado Alley

In the flat heart of tornado alley
each front that slams in spring hangs us
on a thin thread of dread: was this it?

When it got too dark for funnel-spotting
at night we'd still hear the keen of wind,
the hiss of rain on roof. We'd listen then
for the train of trouble. Each shingle

counted for a year.
Dull as death, clouds boil
behind gashes of lightning.
Hail beats even paint from cars.

It hops everywhere, roaring
thick as locusts, bouncing
white marbles on black wet grass.

"Nothing to slow the wind 'tween here
and Canada but barb-wire fences",
they said later, heel-rocking, rough thumbs
hitched up in belt-loops.

Even flat places have a place:
they give a sweeter name to hills.

Goose Hunt

We were laughing and talking quietly
about the effect of temperature on the dissolution
and toxicity of high-velocity lead shot with the air
cold when the far-off geese turned
and came in at us like bombers with their flaps down,
trimming a little left and right.
After the booming smack of the twelve-
gauge guns most scattered but three
fell quickly in short arcs
to the cattails rattling dead in a
sudden ringing silence.

They were heavier than I thought they would be,
wet bodies still warm
and soft. Their long necks
hung limp. With wounded
pride we took our prizes back.
In that bouncing ride with the geese
wrapped in black plastic
I thought about how they came in
wing to wing, strong squadron.
How long will those vacancies
sting in those that left intact?
I cradle that question like a downy body home.

Autumn Blackbirds

7:22 A.M. First
twittering from the dark line of trees
a half mile off

motionless
against pinkening sky.
Then movement

among leaves near the tops of trees,
noise growing, movements
among leaves growing

suddenly a handful of birds
rising,
blackbirds

against gray sky, leaders
bringing the massive flock up,
a noisy swirling cloud

dividing itself
by invisible rules into two,
some moving with the mass north,

some winging hard to make
the mass move south,
stragglers hurrying to join.

Mesa Verde

When we woke and crawled
out of the gray tent, knocking dew, the air
seemed chill as winter. The morning
star hung bright in the east

above the dark ridge but light
permeated enough over the ridge to show
junipers and through this quiet
a flock of more than twenty

wild turkeys worked
systematically yet quickly
among the tents and shrubs
as we stood and watched.

Our small fire among stones was enough
to heat water for coffee and grits,
and our hands, and to send a thin
column of smoke up as we looked

all around for the first time
in Mesa Verde, beautiful
crazy canyon place
we drove to unseeing the night before.

Causality

This afternoon
in luminous light and a cold breeze
straight from the west, six swans

work their huge wings in a line
taking off, beating their way
directly into wind. Their feet

slap the water at first
as they rise straight-necked
an inch at a time.

Branches of a large willow at the pond's edge
move too, but the trunk is fixed—a point of reference
for the rhythmic motion

made now of nothing, constructed
instantaneously
from the stiff wind

and the water-surface
glittering under the arrowing
line of swans, reflecting

light and long-necked determination.

Careful Silence

Alone, late spring, at dusk.
I sit outside sipping a cold beer
in careful silence.

The spiritual atoms of me,
once held together firmly by love or hope,
become charged and slip away

one after another, pulled steadily off.
As they go, some other thing is revealed.
Who or what is this dark thing?

It moves sporadically in me, blind,
trying to become invisible
as I lose myself at night.

Rough Ascension

Loose Image

I would like to go for a walk
or see a movie today, something
to start my life
moving again. It seems stuck

on first, two outs, two strikes,
the batter's blind face is turned to the pitcher,
oak club for a bat waggling
over his shoulder, his ears

tremble for the whistle of ball
coming, skipping the air just as

it vanishes at the last instant, the bat
half through its swing. Buried in this
loose image somewhere silent
as a clown with white circles
smeared around his sad eyes and red
gash of a mouth with the corners

turned down, I live, wanting.

Uncle Eddie Nails the Blues

1.

Uncle Eddie was a fount of knowledge
our mothers didn't like.
He wasn't the uncle of any of us, either.

But with his snaggle-toothed mouth
gnawing the air
he'd spill the beans while his eyes
glittered a smirk on his mouth. He told us

the best way for a man to practice
birth control was to put a small
pebble in his shoe:
guaranteed to make him limp.

And he said the best way for girls
was for them to hold
an aspirin between their knees.

2.

On Fridays when he got drunk enough to sing
he'd stand on the porch
wobble-kneed and belt it out
over the hay-field. Lilacs

could wilt under his whisky-breath
and the full moon
rising seemed to waver. The stubby glass
held Four Roses on a good week.

3.

When he laid down his last
tune and died in spring
it was too early to sing
to a rising moon. We straggled

under a damp day
so far from what he was, pale
sun so thin it scarcely cast a shadow
from one headstone

to the next. And the songs
we sang then were nothing at all
like the ones he sang
teetering on the porch at dark.

Gus Said

Gus said
the doctor said
they need to put
five thin catheters into his boy's heart
tomorrow. One
to feel the pressure; one
for electromagnetic measuring; one
to look through; one
to tell the amount of oxygen
in the blood. And one more

to cut with—
tiny stainless steel scissors
sharp as razors to snip out
bits of bad tissue.
There's nothing those thin tubes won't see
when they start
snaking around
in the young boy's heart.

Gus said the doctor said
cutting's not the issue,
healing is. I said
if I could sing at all
like an angel I would, for him,
and if those slippery tubes came down
wiggling around, looking
in my old blue-black plum, sure, they might see
fear in me, wet and clotted up,
threaded knots of love.

Getting Back

I know nothing but my heart
hammering the dark
sidewalk as I wobble the limits of a weak
pool of light near midnight, the rum
swirly in me, the street
rolling gutter to gutter in a windy
seascape with leaves
scuttering like rats. From this
tippy sidewalk, the rough
edge of being lost scares me.

I try to spell my way back, bleak hotel
rising somewhere
like a mountain under a green
blaze of bronze and glass.
I cross myself, stare up for a star,
work a lean chant. Inside I tilt
at a small angle, perfect as a ring of Saturn.
I search the corner for a street sign,
sniff the air like a dog for north.

Ceremony

This I tell you truthfully occurred
less than a kilometer east of the village Fesi,
near Kpandu, in Ghana, by members
of the Ewe tribe in the lean year
of our Lord, nineteen hundred and seventy six,
by verbal invitation only: being restless,
having recently shaken
free of fever, I went.

Near dusk a small boy
in tattered shorts appeared and led me
downhill on a narrow path into the forest.
Shortly thereafter sunset
plunged us into solid dark
and a dozen wild men began dancing, busy eyes
glinting new fire, ratty hair
long and tangled and thrown about
bare shoulders slicked with sweat,
muscular bodies marked
with ochre, white clay and black,
and oh,

how the drumming went through us—!
The periodic rising and falling
of energy was palpable as
the dancers and drummers
paused to take long drinks
of palm wine from calabash cups, whirring
the dregs in quick arcs
out at us, amazed at the circle's edge watching,
and whenever the dancing fever took pause

the pause was brief and action built again
quickly to a new and higher level.
This secret event went on for hours.

A few old women not engrossed
by watching busied themselves
tending the fires, dragging
big pots of incipient stew to the coals
in pairs or groups of three,
cutting and pitching in
tomatoes, onions, okras, groundnuts,
all manner of things
they knew for a hundred years
belonged in stews until at last

the dancing ended.
The sweaty men
solemn, complete and steady
in palm-wine resolve
got together and dragged in

two bleating black goats roped
by the neck and threw them down,
held them and with their bare feet
killed them, carefully kicking
white ribs into the little dark
warm caverns of life
so as not to spill blood
to the ground.

I still hear the last goat bleating
terrified before the breath went out.

Looking Up

When they rang the bell for the dead man
in the coffin with lilies
casting their heavy scent
in waves, we stood and filed out
to cars in the sun, loading ourselves
with the day, heading
to the cemetery, gravel crunching
under slow tires. Nothing seemed alive
this early in spring. Most of the stones
were slick and prim and new enough
to look hard as granite.

The sod appeared
sullen, dug from its place
and covered with a tarp. I helped
carry the box. We put it
onto straps, and after a few
brief words they lowered it
by cranking into the ground. We stood
at the edge of the blue-striped awning
put up to keep a drizzle at bay.

It was that close
to being wet. My glasses
practically misted from the outside.
It seemed a cloud blew in
from somewhere. Suddenly
there was the sun again and
how could I have missed it,
one small bunch of daffodils blowing
yellow on the hillside, looking up.

Junk-Yard in Spring

So what if through the fence the chromed
ruins of cars rusting in the junk-yard
have the black eyes of knocked-out
windows? Just now I saw a sparrow

slipping from one of those black eyes
looking furtive and thereby
letting me know she was busy
extending her life.

Things I Can Tell My Sons

In 1969 things were in a tizzy
so my brother and I took a summer month
hitch-hiking across the country, backpacks
with sleeping bags cinched on and our thumbs
stuck out, asking for rides. We did it

trying to learn God knows what,
things I guess that make a life
a life. Outside

Coeur D'Alene, across the top of Idaho
on our way east from west, the crystal air
stank of stale smoke and the land
under the pines was tromped and trashed.
We were one day late
for a rock concert, second in size
to Woodstock. Now

approaching noon—a few burned-out hippies
crawling half-asleep from makeshift tents
squatting around a pile of smoking sticks
they called a fire
not knowing what to do. They talked a bit
about maybe looking for weed

to help them wake up. It seemed
a loss to me. Not even oatmeal
for lunch. An hour later we found a sniffling ride
out: Bob, a non-talking bearded guy

tattooed arms big as hams, hairy
knuckles and watery eyes
bounced us in a battered green pick-up truck
twenty miles to town.

Rough Ascension

Eighty years ago an uncle I never knew ascended.
He went up on a bright day rising in a wicker basket
swinging wickedly over a hot blast of smoke,
a darting rush of sparks. Eyes closed, the wind

strokes his black hair, love from a maiden's fingers.
The balloon swells above him,
dark pear of disaster, climbing, angry angel.
Some timeless time later, the young man

steps out between the ropes, bold as bold,
still feeling the wind's caress, coming down
on a clean arc from heaven. When his parachute failed
he hit water drowning, a tangled mess for the casket.

This my tremble-finger dad told me. He confessed
that was the reason he himself could not ascend.
Today I run, working the hard hills, thinking.
It is hot and still. The third hill,

the great Mother Hill of Three-Hill Loop rises,
a moist mirage. Something wavers as sweat drips.
I lean to ascend, breath rising and falling, the dark
cascade of blood rushing like pump-iron squeezing

through my live body. My thoughts become hard
forms with sharp angles; they ascend with me.

Opening a Secret

Under cool leaves on stiff stems
bunches of grapes, individually sweet. Each time
we are surprised to find them—
seedless, fat, pale green globes clinging
tight to the brown cane ready for clipping.
When I push under the shade
opening a secret to the sun it is as though
I am whirled from this Arizona desert
to Greece a thousand years ago.

Chino and I work the long rows together,
clipping the bunches, putting them, stems up,
side by side in wood-slat crates that we lug
to the end of the row. Our sweat
runs out of us and down the bare chest
to the belly-line in the sun.
Soft voices of pickers in other rows
melt to shade. Sometimes
we hide for awhile in leafy tunnels with grapes
hanging by our heads and smoke
bits of clipped brown cane, sitting with our backs
to a box talking quietly in half-light.
Time unwinds slowly
just for us like a high hawk circling.
To the north, mountains unfold in the distance,
blue into blue, wavering.

Today, like many others, trucks get loaded with bright
boxes of fresh grapes. They blap their diesel-smoke
to the air; ready to move
grapes to the cities, grapes to the stores.

Each day, some young part of us
went with the grapes, leaving us older.
On that day, I remember clipping
an inch-long bit of brown cane
like a prayer, tucking it
secretly into a tight bunch
of grapes that went into a box, out of the field,
onto a truck, into the world.

Doing that while imagining grapes
being tended in bright sun
on the stony side of a hill in Greece.

Forty Miles

Forty miles more, the pilot said, and we'll arrive
although by this round window
the city seems closer, spreading like brittle fires
smeared on the dark hills.

An hour later I find myself
driving carefully across the Golden Gate
bridge at night with tensed
bundles of cables thick as an arm
holding me in stasis above water I know
moves in darkness below.

In this place I must think of earthquakes as I drive.
Imagine gas fires roaring through buildings
ripped to chaos, the pallid faces of people
who run or stand in shock.
It seems unlikely that California could fall off
into the ocean, as I've heard said. A physical
impossibility according to the known laws
by which rocks live and hills
seek out their separate shapes.

Well, my love, let me just say this
about travel. It's not all wine and roses.
The getting lost, the quick eye one needs
for street-names, the pulse
high above normal. My briefcase
at least contains familiar things
that comfort me on trips. My whole life
it seems I've been forty miles
away from where I need to be.

Encounter with Deer

Four amber eyes
suddenly in headlights out of the dark, then deer
bodies grow visible standing, one

already leaping
in an instant to kiss the right
shoulder of the car
with her own warm shoulder
pressing
in abrupt love

almost joining

the thumping smack
sends her in a loose tumble
over the car, her eyes
brown as fresh-fallen
oak leaves, her sides busy heaving,

delicate
a small pink
frothy rose grows
redder from her nose.

Nothing we can do
in the glare.
No gun, and even if there was
we could not have used it.

The young boy,
stumbling sleepy from the car's back seat
with one hand
shielding his eyes
from the headlights

keeps asking, what happened
what happened.

Tennessee Heat

1.

The morning opens
virulent as a snake's mouth
in rough pinks and lavenders,
and eleven shades of bleary gray.

It is September: a slender chance
for rain, and that
only if the hurricane
meandering in the gulf
makes up its mind
to punch north hard.

Elemental threads
coming together to weave this day
from beams of early morning light
squeezing from under dry clouds—

Everything brittle as grass.
Sycamores, dogwoods—
the ground has deep cracks,
everything has dried

stiff in heat for weeks.

2.

By noon there is no hope
of rain. Clouds have burned off,
crickets have fallen silent.
I begin looking

for a different way to start
weaving my lonely self
into the day's threads,
seeking a new way to move

past this poisonous
time of dryness.

3.

Trickle of silver
starts from nearly nothing.
I love
my children, my beautiful wife,
whose smooth back
I could scratch for hours,
even our useless dog, deaf
and half blind, sleeping almost motionless

on her favorite crushed-down
dry spot on the front lawn:
her lovely old sides are moving
up and down a little

slowly, in the heat, she's breathing.

Shopping Again

I find myself bringing groceries in
from the truck, loads of things

after shopping: stuffed
into impossibly thin blue plastic bags.

I find myself running out of fingers, hooking
the cut-out handles of the bags, one per finger.

I find there's not enough
fingers, or too many

bags. Lord, there's a gallon of milk
dangling from the pinkie. Chicken,

from the ring-finger; broccoli, carrots, celery
drag the middle finger to pain, the thumb

trembles holding cereal, crackers, a loaf
of bread and cheese is chiefly what I need. These

children I tell you eat and eat
like animals—they'd eat

until the cows come home, then eat
the cows if they could. This eating

goes on each day, all day, and late
into night.

Dissecting Time

Fossils

I come down across stones lightly,
a part of them. Sandstone, shale,
something else that's old-bone white—
perhaps the granite knows.

(The translation of time from stone
to stone
takes time. Things
move slowly.)

Trilobites mix quietly with small fishes.
Coal knows more by far than I.
Anthracite blinks in the sun,
smiling sleepily, thinking deeply of seed-ferns.

There was a time when things
fought to the death to decide
whether a clutch of eggs
would bear scales or feathers.

But now, *Archaeopteryx* is just
a clumsy arrow bent in sandstone,
with a three- or four-chambered heart
that still sighs with your ear held close.

How the Potato Knows*

Four hundred years ago
indigenous farmers in villages
on mountains high in Bolivia and Peru
began forecasting

long-range weather by the stars.
This they do still
by careful observation of the Pleiades
one or two hours before dawn

on multiple nights in June. To the northeast
low in the sky the Pleiades are dimmed
by optically thin cirrus clouds
which increase in El Nino years

relative to drier years
thus, by rainfall, affecting potatoes,
the staple crop, so future yield
formally expressed

becomes correlated to the stars through time.
It works
due to the sensitivity of potatoes to drought.
Yet in this context there is more.

Their multiple eyes seem blind in dirt
but in constant darkness with no rain
in a cupboard within my house
they sprout with a vengeance in spring.

---

*Technical content is from Orlove, B. S. et al. 2000. Forecasting Andean rainfall
and crop yield from the influence of El Nino on Pleiades visibility. *Nature* 403(6):
68–71.

Natural Disaster

I wait patiently for the huge asteroid
unknown to us and with no name
tumbling nonetheless somewhere
through space towards earth,

massive dark rock of destruction,
beast predicted to some day smash us
like the one that carved in an instant
the coast of Yucatán with a vast

fireball cloud of smoke and dust.
I wait patiently for the great quake:
lurch and buckle of land; for the flood,
fire, damning plague, the shiver of shock,

for each great natural disaster that
shakes us loose from who we are
to raise our spirits in a new
conflagration of despair and hope.

Home-Life

1.

Upstairs, beds unmade and clothes
abandoned to the floor—toys, a guitar,
games, shoes, books, all
strewn about, saying

to the parents firmly, do not enter:
this is our place and We
don't want you here, testing
us or meddling

with the slow-developing reptilian
portion of our brains. This is home
for music and incense, for clotted
talk with our teen-age friends.

We circle the mess
daily like old buzzards, snipping edges
and thinking, unlike an old poem, how much
the center holds.

2.

In spring
we break down at last and crack
the windows, letting in fresh air
before starting: then dusting

cobwebs from the corners,
move the dresser, vacuum
old jelly beans from under the bed,
put on new sheets, the whole world

in that one room
swells, ripples, flashes.
Years
fly out, a new time starts.

Ammonite

The flatness of this Oklahoma land
seems propped up
by taut barbed-wire fences protecting
long scraggly lines of weeds

growing under fences, clinging
delicately to a little life.
I walk along a sharp-edged gully cut
two feet deep into the red clay

by last week's rain, feeling
small and alone. Gouged-out,
the gully holds
so many temporary things—stones,

pockets of detritus, clots
of dirt. Suddenly at a bend protruding
from the gully wall, half-buried
bone-white like chalk, big as a small tire wedged

deep under the grass-roots
between the Devonian and the Jurassic
an ammonite fossil, Nautilus-like,
peeks through time, a tight smile.

Waiting for Thunder

1.

Day after day I give myself
up to work. In a mirror
my blurred face, older. Touching
the wrinkles makes me think

of crevasses, ice and thank God the skin
still pulses a little inside.

2.

A cyclone moves on Mars today
licking the red planet's northern cap of ice.
Probably clouds of water-ice, they say.
Probably stirring a little dust.

This, from the Hubble Space Telescope
fresh over the wire on Yahoo dot com.
I blow it up
to grainy perfection.

The thin winds on Mars
I can't see chill me
to perfection at a distance.

3.

This morning
after the first wave of birds
finished singing
I walked barefoot on wet grass

to the fig tree looking for fruits.
They were there
somewhere among the big leaves,
gray-green, starting to swell.

Many small things
cling quietly to leaves or hang
from finger-fat stems
gray in the half-light of dawn,
wet and alive.

4.

When I was five I remember
the neighbor's boy in coveralls
almost a man helping his dad on Saturday
catch an alligator snapper, big as a dinner-plate
and a bit more besides. In the wet ditch
under trees with an old broom,

offering the wood
handle to his slashing jaws, the boy
on the straw end, the man

gingerly lifting the distal end. The stinking
thing too big for its shell;
the penile neck wrinkly and the dangerous head

whipping, at last biting the wood. They lifted,
the neck stretched, the snapper's weight
made the broom handle sag.

That day the boy and the dad and the grandad too
said, sure a snapper won't never let go
til it thunders—that was a fact.

But he made a fine soup the next day
with potatoes, thunder or no.
I think now a whole life can be spent OK

giving up love, waiting for thunder.

Summer Job

For two full summer days I shovel
crap and straw from a hen-house floor,
ammonia reeking the air
acrid as a jungle flower gone mad.

With each push the shovel slides
under the mess scraping
concrete, green juice dribbling
darker than spinach and all the while

white chickens
frightened or pretending fright, inspect
progress, look
for worms or maggots or whatever else

gets turned up. They blink
their eyes and cock their heads, high-step
the straw, strut up
wood planks to their nest-boxes

nailed to the wall. Close overhead the sheet-
metal roof and between the roof and the wall
wire mesh through which comes sun
pale from passing through leaves and dust.

Looking back,
the wheelbarrow-work was hardest,
plunging me from shadowed shed
to full sun blazing like a hammer,

the top-heavy thing wobbling
fifty yards to the garden,
there dumped in a concluding hasty rush.
The worn wood handles lifted

smooth to the touch when I moved and the air
was for an instant cool moving past
blueberry bushes whispering
a secret. The air said, don't think

about sweat or straw-juice,
dribbling or stench: it's OK.
This is your summer job.

In Their Time

As a young child he resurrected birds from the dead.
They shook themselves alive and sprang into the air
frightened but glad to live again.

    Somewhere, I once read
that less than two nanoseconds after the Big Bang
all physical laws of the universe had already
leaped out of the incredible

spark of nothing to hold
center stage full-blown: the jester's
two-toned hat had bells, the bull's
big balls hung to his hairy knees.

Uncertainty crept in. Pan began looking
for lost pipes while Pandora wrote
and rewrote the script for patience.
Athena worked in her kitchen baking bread;

she was kneading and kneading the dough to learn Zen
when suddenly she came to an ecstatic state of
enlightenment and everything began running
backwards, spilling time into the aisles,

making hills, then mountains, of chaos.
In dreamland I recreate the universe:
I begin putting things gently into their places
one by one; a long night, I tell myself:

all things will come in their time.

Oklahoma Radio

Radio waves skip
ethereal, silent over the grassy hills
racing sunlight, dodging hollows as I drive

a steady pace, listening
carefully for messages in the rock of rock.
Beatles give me
hey Jude, here comes the sun.

Outside, a boy on a dirt-bike
snarls up a torn hill while radio waves dance
like heat: through, under, around him.
Focused on the hill, handlebars, throttle,

he clutches in and shifts
as Chicago whispers by, hurtling north
towards Tulsa, spawned
in eerie silence in Dallas, Tex.

The crackle of NPR waxes and wanes
as I crest hills and sink through valleys.
I am on the edge of nowhere,
catching moon-bounce:

the ancient sizzle of cosmic noise,
beautifully mixed
with Sousa, Bach
and Charlie Pride.

Contrary Ecologist

Advances in ecology, like advances in other domains of human activity, occur unevenly: they emerge erratically and unexpectedly, in a series of fits and starts. Often, these advances begin with the development of a new tool—a new modeling approach, for example, or the demonstration of a new type of measuring device, or a novel means for characterizing some previously difficult-to-estimate process or state. Examples of new tools that have allowed ecological science to lurch forward include the ability to produce and measure various radioactive and stable isotopes suitable for use as sensitive tracers of elemental and biochemical pathways; high-performance, low-cost computers, which allowed the development of process modeling and encouraged wide-spread use of statistical analyses. More recent examples of such tools include PCR (polymerase chain reaction), DNA microarrays, microcantilever-based sensor devices, and multispectral and even hyperspectral laser-induced detection and ranging (Lidar) instruments. Each of these techniques is now on the verge of irrevocably changing the way in which ecologists investigate and thus come to understand the natural world.

There is something about the erratic flurry and fizzle of techno-logical progress characterizing these great intermittent lurches for-ward that interests me almost as much as the advances themselves. For example, how, exactly, are new technologies incorporated into ecology? And are the pathways by which these technologies become firmly incorporated similar to each other, or highly variable? Surely none of the new technologies spring forth upon the ecological landscape, precocial, full-blown and feathered! And after a given technology has emerged and matured, and is done providing the in-formation that was desired—what then? Does it recede through time towards extinction, perhaps wavering a bit at the last, something like a mirage of bones on a high thin desert? The catastrophic overturning of conceptual paradigms described years ago by Thomas Kuhn in his book *The Structure of Scientific Revolutions* may be similar to the process whereby technologies enter, dominate for a time, then fade from favor.

I think about these things while driving slowly home from work in my 1995 Ford Ranger pickup truck. The truck is hunter green on the outside, with an extended cab and a narrow bed. The bed is lined with hard black plastic, deeply ridged—a technological marvel, 30 years ago. Inside, a pair of pull-down jump-seats is in the back, and there is gray carpeting all around, but through time the gray-carpeted floor by the driver's seat has become ringed and slopped with coffee. I clean it periodically, working the stains experimentally with various materials—Resolve®, or Mr. Clean®, or water with just a drop of soap—they all seem to do about the same. Scrub in, froth up, allow it to stand a moment, then wipe away. Two days later the next spill happens. On the dashboard is Leslie, Comma, The Navigating Mouse.

Leslie, Comma, The Navigating Mouse is made of a rubbery plastic. He's an odd little creature, to be sure—a greenish white base color, with the back and the tops of the paws being greener than the lighter belly. On the head, between the two small red-dot eyes is a blue patch, and behind that, between the cunning ears, is a sprayed-on little patch of yellow. Leslie, Comma, The Navigating Mouse is about three inches long, from the tip of his plastic-whiskered nose to the base of the tail. The whiskers are six in number, three on each side. They are short, and stick straight out—not too interesting. But the tail—! That's a good six inches in length. It tapers gradually all the way from the rump to the tip, and is banded elegantly in alternating patches of yellow and blue. Leslie, Comma, The Navigating Mouse generally is placed just so, on the dashboard of the truck, to peer forward through the windshield. When children ride with me in the truck I tell them that Leslie, Comma, The Navigating Mouse, by looking forward, guides our progress, and thereby gets us to where we want to go. Every ecologist needs a Leslie, Comma, The Navigating Mouse. Every ecologist needs an icon or two, to get along.

Ecologists as a group are busy now transforming themselves into something new. Just yesterday, it seems, we were hunter-gatherers, hard-eyed individuals sniffing the landscape with flared nostrils, wandering hither and yon, abstracting a bit of this, a little of that, snippets of data on the autecology of nondescript creatures in grasslands, lakes and streams, and at the forest's edge.

We studied sand-dunes and the tendency of fish to move
with flow, the population dynamics of goldenrod,
teasel, lupine, geckos, whip-tail lizards,
scissors-tail flycatchers, foxes,

those capable
and incapable of flying,
indeed an entire suite
of wet, dry and wiggly things.

Now suddenly it seems
each day the sun rises a bleary slab
of orange or pink under a smear of clouds. I think
yes, we really should give homage

to Santa Rosalia: we really should
bow and give thanks
to Our Sacred Sister, the long-haired
Sweet Lady of Perpetual Notion.

Unquestionably, as a tribal group, ecologists have become agrarian. We have become users of larger-scale data: from well-planned work farmed out now in perfect rows, lush results are mowed, raked in, piled up, all but baled. We are in the process of becoming more integrative in thought and deed; we work now more in collaborative teams than as isolated individuals; we listen more closely to the hark and call of programmatic themes outlined by potential sponsoring agencies. We have become, in a bleak sense, harvesters of sterile data flowing in from large areas.

We Are Defined

by the blind eyes of satellites
cast into geocentric orbit;
by the flux of data, slippery
element of truth. It is no accident

the rose
suddenly has made up its mind to bloom:
blood put to the soil 20 years ago
has done its job.

The technologies collectively encouraging the conversion of ecologists from hunter-gatherers into members of an ecological agrarian society are in many cases the same technologies that allow us as humans to see the earth more holistically. This grand metamorphosis puts us into the position where just to survive professionally we must learn.

We Must Learn

each day again to drink
from a fire-hose. When we have finished
with this earth
or it more likely is finished with us

this evening, at the sweet crepuscular hour
of early summer, the blessed time
when single fireflies rise in silence
on steady wings

into the soft air between the white pines,
the special trees that grow
near the linden tree we planted
knowing

in our hearts at least we will die
later in some bleak winter of discontent
before any of these trees have reached
their proper stately age of life

the voice I offer in this dusk
moves out, comes back empty;
it does not seem to be enough.

Much subtle confusion accompanies the more-than-technical metamorphosis of hunter-gatherer ecologists to an agrarian ecological society, in every area of ecological research. A simple example, dug shallowly from personal experience, is instructive of this point. We know, from numerous studies, many of the benefits that the cryptic endophyte, *Neotyphodium*, provides its host, tall fescue, a forage grass now planted deliberately across tens of thousands of acres in the United States, under names such as 'Kentucky 31.' The host plant is rendered more drought-tolerant and cold hardy, more able to grow on low-nutrient soil, and less suitable as forage for ungulate and invertebrate grazers as a result of the endophyte's presence. But what, exactly, are we to do with such information, now that we have it? And of perhaps greater significance, now knowing what we know, what is the appropriate driver for acquiring any additional knowledge on this topic, or virtually any other?

Several years ago the phrase "pattern and process" was all the rage in ecology, having been expressed clearly by an eminent few in thematic talks at societal meetings and in studies published in reputable ecological journals. And with this encouragement and compass-point for progress, the younger and less eminent of those among us began redefining the ecological world around us comfortably in terms of pattern and process—a compelling demonstration of the yin and yang of an ecologically robust creative energy turned loose, gone wild. It seems to me now, sitting here safely in my soft chair, that we are constantly desperate for leaders, good or bad. And this desire to be led, rather than step forth to lead, is as strong in the sciences as it is in every other aspect of our nubby little individual lives. This flaw, if a flaw it is, is so deeply rooted in the self that we can see scarcely far enough to discern a pattern.

If a pattern existed—even if
it stood to its full three-inch height and bit
one on the butt. It seems

each of us is hiding
in a fox-hole of our own making.
Peering

over the rocky edge
occasionally
we can see

the eyes of another,
frightened too.

It is not easy to crawl out of a foxhole, especially one of our own making. There are, after all, dangerous things flying around out there, and it seems so much safer here, squatting, even if it is dark and a bit wet. An unusual level of something—let's call it courage, or curiosity, perhaps—is needed to cause one to emerge, just for the purpose of beginning to explore places and things unknown. So thank God for rationalization! It is the only force, I suspect, that is greater than the force of fear or greed. We can always find good reasons for doing what we choose to do, and firm reasons for not doing what we chose to avoid.

And here, practically by accident, I find I have at last blundered into the center of the thing that gnawed me into writing this eclectic, hodge-podge essay: the concept of belief systems, a notion that links the mythologies of plastic mice, emerging technologies, and the inexorable transformation of ecologists from individual hunter-gatherers into a more collective, agrarian scientific society. It is, in particular, the idea that each person chooses, consciously or unconsciously, to modify his or her belief system, so as to rationalize into practical existence the relative strengths and weaknesses of various lines of evidence that the individual uses subsequently to guide his or her own actions. These self-constructed multiple lines of evidence of course are invisible; they are established in part by logic, in part by happenstance, and in part by a deep-rooted desire to ascribe causality to a comfortable cause-and-effect reality, a satisfying pattern-and-process structure. Yet it seems clear, too, that these lines of fuzzy logic meander, occasionally reinforcing one another, occasionally conflicting. The construct is a convoluted net of our own making, ultimately functioning much like a foxhole. We use these lines to establish a web that defines and protects us, at least in part, from the painful little vagaries of day-to-day life. Many of the lines, with their individual kinks and curls, we construct early in life, as children, from a child's point of view. And often it is easier just to carry these along, woven in, than it is to pull them out, prune out the dead tendrils, undo the kinks of the useful living stems, and take the time to re-weave them more thoughtfully into a neater, stronger, more adult-like structure. We are, after all, mythologically organic at our roots—so damn them! Let the dead vines lie! Fungi take us, and bugs, and rot! A leaf dies? So, let it! Surely it will mulch another. And so we should not be surprised when a pale thigmotrophic tendril originating from a 30- or 40-year-old stem occasionally slips up, touches the face at night, cool and soft, curls the ear, whispering

> I am green but not real.
> Nothing
> I say to you
> should be held to the heart.
> Listen.

At last, I derive comfort from the idea that my own metamorphosis might be possible, even if improbable. I think I am starting to believe that it is OK to muddle through life—after all, do we have a choice? Perhaps, I think, it truly is impossible for someone to shed their leafy sheath, once it has been built, so as to let the vines and their trembling attendant leaves fall to the sides, letting the inner human form rise, Psyche-like, naked, individual, and beautifully transcendent. But as a contrary ecologist I also know it is possible to retain a spark of that glowing light of curiosity, manifest in child-wonder—the spark of wonder capable of pulling us out: the lovely glow that moves erratically and so enticingly, over there, just a bit beyond the edge of the foxhole. The bit of light, there, moving, practically calling from the darkness—there, do you see it?

About the Author

Arthur Stewart is an ecologist, senior scientist, essayist and poet. He graduated from Agua Fria Union High School and Northern Arizona University (B.S. and M.S. degrees) before spending two years as a Peace Corps Volunteer in Ghana. Upon returning to the U.S., he completed a Ph.D. in limnology at Michigan State University and a postdoctoral fellowship at the Department of Energy's Oak Ridge National Laboratory, in Oak Ridge, Tennessee. He taught aquatic ecology and conducted stream-ecology studies as an Assistant Professor at the University of Oklahoma for three years before returning to Oak Ridge National Laboratory to work as an aquatic ecologist and ecotoxicologist. He has authored or coauthored more than sixty articles and book chapters, and has served as editor or associate editor for *Environmental Toxicology and Chemistry, Journal of the North American Benthological Society*, and *Ecotoxicology*. He is an Adjunct Research Professor at the University of Tennessee, and lives in Lenoir City. *Rough Ascension and Other Poems of Science* is his first book of poetry.